Bad Auditions

A Smith and Kraus Book
177 Lyme Road, Hanover, NH 03755
editorial 603.643.6431 To Order 1.877.668.8680
www.smithandkraus.com

Bad Auditions
Copyright © 2017 by Julia Duffy

All rights reserved.

Manufactured in the United States of America

CAUTION: Professionals and amateurs are hereby warned that the material represented in this book is subject to a royalty. It is fully protected under the copyright laws of the United States of America, and of all countries covered by the International Copyright Union (including the Dominion of Canada and the rest of the British Commonwealth), and of all countries covered by the Pan-American Copyright Convention and the Universal Copyright Convention, and of all countries with which the United States has reciprocal copyright relations. All rights, including professional, amateur, motion picture, recitation, lecturing, public reading, radio broadcasting, television, video or sound taping, all other forms of mechanical or electronic reproductions such as information storage and retrieval systems and photocopying, and the rights of translation into foreign languages, are strictly reserved.

ISBN: 9781575259208
Library of Congress Control Number: 2017959937

Typesetting and layout by Elizabeth E. Monteleone
Cover photo by: John Palmieri

For information about custom editions, special sales, education and corporate purchases, please contact Smith and Kraus at editor@smithandkraus.com or 603.643.6431.

Printed in the United States of America

BAD AUDITIONS

Julia Duffy

S&K

SMITH AND KRAUS   2018

For Fran Bascom

"If you get a chance to act in a room that somebody else has paid rent for, then you've been given a free chance to practice your craft."
Philip Seymour Hoffman

Table Of Contents

Introduction	11
Foreword	15
Bad Audition #1	19
Ignore The Stage Directions	
Bad Audition #2	25
The Interview, Or Please Just Let Me Act	
Bad Audition #3	31
How Old Do You Want Me To Be?	
Bad Audition #4	35
Sometimes It's Best To Read With The Casting Person	
Bad Audition #5	41
I Got The Part Anyway	
Bad Audition #6	47
The Printer Ate My Sides	
Bad Audition #7	51
How I Managed To Blow A Self-Tape	
The Waiting Room:	57
Welcome To Purgatory	
In The Room:	61
Choose Your Adventure	

Oh Crap, They Want A Monologue   67
Dealing With Frustration,   73
   Or Why Didn't I Get The Part??
Self Tapes: 79
   You Should Still Get Nervous
My Best Audition   85
   or What a Difference the Casting Person Can Make
Dear 20-Year Old Me: 91
   Regrets And Wisdom
Epilogue   99
Acknowledgements   103
Afterword   109
About the Author   115

Introduction

Not long ago I was preparing to address a group of young thespians. As I went over the points I wanted to make about starting out in our business—such as handling nerves, what real commitment is when assuming a role and how to best achieve it—I had a revelation. I realized every time I illustrated a point from an experience in my own life, it was often in relation to an audition—either concerned with what occurred at one, or when preparing for it. My epiphany (not an entirely welcome one) reminded me that so much of my career consisted of the audition experience.

Some of these experiences seem even more deeply ingrained in my memory than the actual jobs. Many were events of great substance, epics that played out over a few days of intense preparation culminating in five minutes of great success or failure, and almost always an exponential amount of learning about the business, my creative process, and of course my own actor's psyche.

It is sobering to realize auditions comprised my body of work, as much as the real work. My auditions are what directors and producers remember. I have no doubt there are many people whose impression of me is still rooted in what they saw me do, or fail to do, in a few minutes, in a poorly lit office, decades, months, or perhaps weeks ago.

One audition keeps cropping up in my memory, and though it occurred around forty years ago, it will not go away. I used to tell people this story, when the conversation turned to such things, as a way of pointing out how wildly unpredictable the audition business can be.

I was reading for an independent film about two teenage lovers, innocents. There were a number of great two-person scenes between the young leads but I was told to just read the script and go in, don't prepare anything. Upon arriving, I noted the casting woman treated me warmly in the waiting area as she told me how much the director had loved the ingénue star of his previous film—let's call her Gina. That film was another coming-of-age story, in which this Gina had made a big splash and instantly became the go-to girl for sweet young thing roles. The casting woman said her director was very proud of having discovered Gina and clearly hoped lightning would strike for him again with this new film. The chatty casting woman then sighed and said "you're so perfect for this role, but I warn you, he really prefers brunettes." You may now guess what color Gina's hair was.

I was then led into the audition room where the director greeted me and studied me closely as we talked. Very soon he mentioned his previous film, and how wonderful Gina was and I hastened to agree, though I had yet to see it. He chose a scene for us to read together in which the boy had what amounted to a page long monologue, with the girl responding with a few lines near the end of the scene. He said what he was really looking for was someone who could listen, really *listen*, because this boy was being listened to for the first time in his life, and that's why he falls

Bad Auditions

in love with her. I nodded intently, to show him how passionately I was now *listening*.

He began to read. He started to read the boy's long speech, struggling to both read and glance up at me between lines, to catch how well I was, you know, *listening*, and then, after just two lines of the speech said "mm, ok, blah blah . . ." and then skipped to the last line of the monologue. Skipping nearly a page of dialogue to which I was supposed to be, well, *listening*.

Now I suppose at some point he may have thought, no, no blonde just won't do, she's just not Gina, and trusting his own stellar instincts chose not to waste any more time on someone who was just not *her*. (And I will discuss the existence of Svengali-like directors later.)

What could I have done? Besides spending forty years thinking of this as the apocryphal audition story, a great illustration of what we as actors are up against and the utter unfairness of it all? Well, I could have done something. There were things within my power that could have maximized the impression I made in those five minutes. I could have seen the movie he directed, it was currently in theatres, and it might have told me much about how he had cast previously and what his sensibilities were. I could have chosen several scenes to work on despite being told it was just a meeting. Thus prepared I might have been able to ask if I could do one of them. At the very least if I had committed to working on some pivotal scenes, even without the opportunity to do them, I may have begun to have a strong feel for the character that would have been useful even in a truncated audition. I had enough training, enough experience playing that type of role, that some prep coupled with both the casting director and director's cues should have been sufficient to allow me to bring some of the girl's quality into my few moments with him, and even to the few lines he had me say. Had I done everything in my power to connect with the script and character it may be that a glimmer of the character would have penetrated his thick skull and he might have moved on to a scene that more fully showcased the girl.

And this brings me to my point, and the reason I offer my experiences, however humiliating, to the young actor to ponder: most directors and casting people are pros. However, you WILL encounter less than conducive situations, and you must keep in mind whether they are hardened veterans or less-than-pro newbies, they have never cast *that* role before. The expert in the room is you. What they may fail to bring to the process you can provide. Help them cast the role, make them see what they need to see. Though it's rare to encounter someone as lame at conducting an audition as the above-mentioned director, it does happen. Learn from my auditions, especially the bad ones. Forty years is just too long to wait to realize what you should have done at an audition.

Julia Duffy

Foreword

It's safe to say that most auditions are bad auditions. The process is painful, stressful, humiliating, and soul crushing. In any session, no matter how many actors audition, at best only one person will get the part. It is a fool's endeavor, a kamikaze mission, a setup for failure, likely to leave the actor lost and rejected, often even after a brilliant performance. But it is also an inevitable and necessary part of the job, so it is essential for every actor to find some comfort in the process.

What Julia has written here is both a series of tremendously entertaining anecdotes from her own audition experiences, and a wise, insightful guide for the actor. If you're reading this, you must already have some inkling of how terrific a performer Julia Duffy is. I've only had the pleasure of working with her once, on a memorably tricky series of Thanksgiving scenes for the TV show 'Scream Queens.'

Julia had been cast as the matriarch in a truly deplorable old-moneyed American family. I had not been involved in her audition for the show, but I knew her work and was looking forward to seeing what she might bring to the table. The Thanksgiving table. With no less than 8 principal players. Such scenes are endlessly tedious, technically challenging, physically and mentally taxing, and absolutely horrendous for both actors and directors because of the relentless repetition. Julia, no surprise, was a marvel. She came with a fully-thought-out approach to the character, played it with commitment and skill, and managed to be dry, funny, satirical, frightening, and authentic, all at the same time. Over and over again. And patient. And flexible. And generous to her fellow performers.

I promise you, this woman knows what she's doing. You'll do well to pay close attention to everything she says. When I spend time socializing with actors, the subject almost inevitably turns to auditions. Who auditioned for what, who else was there, how horrible the room was, how stressful it was, how great or how bad the audition in general went— this provides endless material for conversations among actors who, oddly and without exception, find no greater pleasure than talking about themselves and their work.

Ask an actor about their worst professional experience, and it's likely to have happened in an audition. Ask them about their best experiences, and you'll learn there are few greater highs than to walk out of an audition knowing you've nailed it. Whether you get the part or not is, of course, another story. If you want to know more about Julia's highs and lows, read this book. Auditions are the bane of every actor's professional life. I don't know a single performer who professes to enjoy auditions.

Oh, wait, that's not true. Just last week an actor told me that he'd finally figured out a way to let go, to accept the random nature of the universe, to surrender himself to the gods of fate and to actually be happy about auditioning. He told me that he now enjoyed the audition process more than the final acting work itself. He had found true joy in putting himself up for judgment, knowing that it was simply another chance to hone things and another chance to perform. And, as every actor will tell you, the opportunity to perform, to ply the craft, is what it's all about. He truly seemed a peace with himself and with the most painful part of his profession. I was impressed.

Is he a saint, a wise, patient, self aware sage? Perhaps a Buddhist? No. Further probing revealed that he was comfortable auditioning ONLY because of his secure job as the lead in a successful streaming show that was guaranteed a long run. I promise you, once that show is canceled (they all end sooner or later, except, apparently, The Simpsons), he will go back to loathing each and every aspect of the audition.

In the meantime, between his happy-go-lucky auditions, he should read this book. Julia's book was, for me, a long series of 'aha' moments. As a director, I've spent much of my professional life sitting on the other side of the audition room. It is almost as painful to sit through auditions as it is to audition. Well, maybe not almost, but it can be emotionally difficult. My heart goes out to every performer who comes into the room. More so to the ones who are well prepared and willing to put everything out there to get cast. Which is most actors.

We want them to be great. We want them to amaze us. We want them to do things we'd never expect in the role. And as director I want them to do it again, differently, even if they did it beautifully the first time; I need to know how an actor takes direction and makes an adjustment. After they're done, I want to hug them, tell them how great they are, and apologize right then and there for not giving them the part, in spite of their tremendous talents and efforts. But I don't. It's usually "thank you so much, you did great," and on to the next.

Julia Duffy

But if sitting on the other side of the audition room can be painful, it is still far easier to be the one who is involved in the choosing a rather than be the one trying to be chosen or positively judged. Every director, casting director, producer, and studio head should read this book. If you're an actor, you'll benefit hugely from reading this book. It'll help you in more ways than you expect. If you like to watch plays, movies or television, you'll love Julia's insights into the actor's process—and if you don't like watching these things, for God's sake put this down and read a self-help book. If you're a professional in the performing arts, any aspect, listen to everything Julia has to say. Her stories are entertaining, amusing, frightening, and filled with insight into the actor's art. If you care about acting for any reason, you should read this book. I promise you'll be glad you did.

Michael Lehmann

Michael Lehmann has been a director and producer in film and television for over thirty years. After studying philosophy at Columbia University and the University of Tübingen in Germany, Lehmann got his start in the movies as receptionist for Francis Coppola's Zoetrope Studios in San Francisco. He went on to attend the USC School of Cinema TV and has since directed nine feature films and over ninety episodes of television. His films include *Heathers*, *Airheads*, and *The Truth About Cats and Dogs*, and in television he's directed, among others, episodes of *The West Wing, Homicide, The Larry Sanders Show, Californication, Dexter, True Blood, American Horror Story,* and *Scream Queens*. In spite of this vast experience, he's still looking forward to his first audition as an actor.

Bad Audition #1

Or Ignore the Stage Directions

The ingénue years begin.

Bad Auditions

Recently I read for a pilot written by a well known, very edgy comedy writer. The role was of a seemingly mild mannered middle-aged housewife, whose fortunes had fallen severely. She and her husband were now living in the basement of their home while their sons were living upstairs. Her husband had lost his job and all their money, but their sons were able to make the house payments the parents could no longer afford. She was bitter underneath but sweet to everyone—almost every line had a direction like "said with absolute sincerity," or "sweetly." I assumed they would build up to an episode where she would finally lose it and spew venom in a shocking moment. But in this pilot script she's unrelentingly sweet.

Soon after I arrived an actress I know came in, dressed beautifully in an expensive looking outfit. I laughed and said well, one of us is dressed wrong. I had on a shirt and pants, as such a point had been made in the script of how much they'd lost, and that they had sold so many of their possessions. I was called in first, the audition was on camera, and only the casting person was in the room. I read the role as I'd prepared, lots of undercurrents, but always sweet and deferential to whomever the character was addressing.

The casting person said great, now do it again with absolutely no sweetness, the writer wants her to be dripping with bitterness, vicious. Well, I found it nearly impossible, I had been so influenced by the directions, and her direction did not mesh with the dialogue at all. I did it again, trying to find this radically different attitude. She then said to do it again, even nastier. I did my best but I was thrown, and ashamed of myself for letting this audition get so out of my control.

When I left, and was gathering my things I heard the next auditioner and realized if one was sitting near the door everything said in the room could be heard. And the actress I knew—the one dressed beautifully—was sitting next to the door. She would have heard everything the casting person said to me. She's a very good actress but has never played sweet and never will. She's excellent and funny at being cool, bitchy, snobby, and always plays someone upper class. In fact, when she first walked in I found it odd that she was there. She got the part.

What could I have done? Well, once I found out how differently they wanted the role played than I had rehearsed I could easily have asked to go out and come back in, saying I needed a few minutes to adjust. She might have said no but probably would have said yes, and I was remiss not to ask.

But what happened is hardly without precedent and I should have practiced what I preach to young actors: rehearse it in *different* ways. Not only will you be more ready when something is thrown at you, but in the process of trying something different it is very possible you will find different colors, more depth, even entirely new insights into the character that can help your original take on the role as well. I rely on my instincts, they have served me well, but I can rely on my instincts and go that extra mile too. It can only help, it's the professional thing to do, and in this case, would have made an enormous difference.

All of your training and experience should be used for each audition, and a script as funny and complex as this one deserved more exploration. For instance, I should have realized that the middle-age character had enjoyed a successful like until very recently, and what she WAS, prior to this time, needed to be evident. True, if they were looking for the character to be played exactly as described, I would not now be faulting my preparation.

I don't know where the disconnect occurred between what was written and how it was cast, but stage directions or not, there was complexity to the character and I should have responded to it by going beyond my first instincts. And I think I should have worn a dress. Yeah. Definitely should have worn a dress.

BAD AUDITION #2

The Interview, or Please Just Let Me Act

Still an ingénue.

Bad Auditions

During the ridiculously lengthy ingénue phase of my career, I was asked to come in "just to meet" an amazing number of times. Later it would make a little more sense, when the director and casting people were familiar with my work, but I found it so strange when I was completely unknown that a director would just want to sit and talk to me as opposed to having me perform a scene.

I will go out on a limb here and say I doubt it happens to men nearly as often. In fact, I will be very blunt and say I believe casting any sort of young, romantic female role brings out the Svengali in some male directors [no doubt young male actors sometimes encounter something similar as well]. I'm not even sure they're always aware of this, it's part of their creative process and usually not anything like overt flirting. [And if that occurs, it should be reported to your agent, and maybe the union.]

Even very recently I experienced something that falls into this category. I read for a wonderful role of a lonely, neglected and stir-crazy housewife, and I was, at that time, just the right age for it, and the same age exactly as the already-cast husband. At the first audition the director—really a very nice guy—talked to me for a while about the play and the role. While describing the quality most important to him he said "I don't care if she's twenty-five or forty-five, she must have that longing, lonely quality."

I couldn't help myself-I said "twenty-five?? She's been isolated for a very long time, and then her husband would be something like thirty years older!" He demurred, saying he was just illustrating the point. The reading however went very well and I was called back. There was only one other actress waiting. She was very pretty and very much younger than me. Very much. She got the role.

Now, I had intended not to sound bitter in this book, but I mention this particular audition not to point out what I could have done differently, but simply to include all the things that may happen to influence a casting choice. There are male directors—and possibly female, but of course I've worked with fewer of them—who need to fall a little bit in love to cast certain roles. Just as it helps you in a romantic role to find your co-star attractive, so too does it often help the director to find an actor appealing, and what he or she finds appealing is going to be, by its nature, subjective.

I believe the above story helps explain why some directors want to "just meet." I assume they have great confidence in their powers of perception about an actor, and particularly when casting a role that's a romantic ideal of some sort I guess they need to "feel" something. And this isn't limited to roles that require sex-appeal, a director is often searching for a strong quality in many kinds of roles and seeks to discover an actor that embodies it from the moment they walk in the door.

Figuring out how to project this ephemeral quality is something I never mastered, and here's an example of that failure: I had an audition for a small but important indy film about a group of friends and their escapades and romances over a period of several years. I had the script but no further instructions, so I worked on several of the biggest scenes. However, upon arriving I discovered they just wanted to talk. There were two of them, a director and producer, very young guys who were becoming a hot duo after their first film, which was completed but not yet out.

I hoped we'd discuss the script, which I very much liked, but their conversation quickly turned away from that. They began discussing their last movie, and made jokes and gossiped, quite outrageously, about the well-known leading man they'd just worked with. I had no idea if I was to participate in this talk or not. The role I was up for was a vulnerable young woman, a late bloomer, a bit of an outsider in the group. I chose to behave more like the role and be rather quiet. I felt more and more awkward, sitting in an uncomfortable, oversized chair. I can't recall how the meeting ended, only that it seemed to last forever and I was in that damn chair with no exit strategy. Later that day the casting person called my agent and asked if I was okay. My agent asked why and she said "Well, they said she just sat there slumped down in the chair and seemed 'weirded out'."

What could I have done differently? Anybody? Well, I'll never know what would have made it a successful interview from their point of view. But I do believe they needed to feel that I was cool, fun, and their kind of chick to work with. It's a very personal thing for a director to choose someone he's going to be working closely with for weeks, and I feel now that I needed to reveal more of myself and do what I could to insert myself into the give and take of the conversation.

Their script may have been very personal to them and they likely saw their own youthful experiences in it. I don't find their attitude in the room very admirable, but this was *their* movie. They were the ones I needed to impress, and what they needed from me was to be more forthcoming and make them see I could be part of their group. The difficult truth: it's their right to conduct the casting process however they see fit and our job is to go with the flow, even when they make it hard to do so.

I should have asked questions, shown interest, and taken it upon myself to make the meeting meaningful, rather than wait for them to give me cues. They probably had no idea how off-putting their behavior was, or what most meetings are like for actors. Sure, they were full of themselves, but as I say, it was their movie. If I had to shoulder 98% of the effort to make the meeting fruitful then that was my job.

Maybe they needed to find the actress personally appealing, needed to imagine her as someone to fall in love with, or maybe they just wanted to feel she was their kind of chick, but clearly, when they choose just talking over reading a scene, it's important to reveal yourself. Some directors trust their guts and, like Woody Allen, never audition. It may seem odd and vaguely unprofessional, but this type of meeting is part of our job.

BAD AUDITION #3

Or How Old Do You Want Me to Be?

Who talked me into this pose?

Bad Auditions

Sometimes you just can't win. When I was in my twenties I looked like a teenager. I looked so young I was being rejected for roles of 18 and 19 year olds. As the years went by I became conflicted about what I should say when asked how old I was. I felt it influenced people unduly and of course I didn't want to hand them a reason to reject me. So, when I was given the opportunity to audition for a great role in an off-Broadway play of a fourteen-year-old girl, I decided to lie. I didn't feel they would cast someone anywhere near fourteen, someone that young wouldn't have the maturity to understand the play, which was full of imagery and metaphor. But if I said my age-twenty-four-I was sure they'd be unable to imagine me in the role.

The audition went very well and when they asked how old I was I said nineteen. I figured that was old enough to grasp the nuance of the role but young enough that they would feel confident I'd be believable as fourteen. I got a callback, which also went well. After I finished, the director and producer sat silently for a moment, looking thoughtful. Finally, one of them said "We really like you, it's just . . . you're so young, and this play requires a great deal of maturity to fully understand."

I was frozen for a moment, somehow too afraid to admit I'd lied, wondering if now they would believe me, after having lied. I tried to remember if my driver's license was in my purse so I could prove I'd been lying. But they then thanked me, and I had no choice but to walk out the door, and I did so in the most grown-up way I could. I did not get the role.

Well, obviously, I should have spoken up and said my real age, and not have worried so much about admitting my previous lie. What were they going to do, call the truth police? In that instance, perhaps the contrast between my real-life demeanor and that of the young girl I had just portrayed would have been helpful, they could have seen both the adequate maturity needed for the job, and my ability to completely take on a more youthful essence. In this case, they would have felt more comfortable knowing I was accomplished at acting young, as opposed to being young.

But of course, you never know.

BAD AUDITION #4

Or Sometimes It's Better to Read with the Casting Person

*Obligatory fan blowing the hair.
It was the 80s.*

Bad Auditions

During the run of a highly successful, offbeat series on cable, I was called into read for a guest role four different times. The first three times I was far too young and each of those times the role was cast with an actress who was, or looked to be, ten to fifteen years older than me. I felt I wasn't doing myself any good, being seen time after time for roles I was dead wrong for. The show often had interesting, very worthwhile guest roles that I felt I'd never get a chance to read for due to this misperception of me that was apparently stuck in someone's mind.

Then finally I was called in to read for a charming role that seemed to fit me physically and age-wise. This time the star of the show wanted to read with me and I was treated very nicely. I had to wait a while as he was on the set shooting a scene. Finally, the actor came running into the casting office, wearing his costume [pajamas], said a quick and friendly hello, and scanned the sides quickly. He was clearly unfamiliar with the scene and began reading while trying to find the correct blocking. Normally an already cast actor would read off-camera, just as the casting person would, but not him. He stepped into the shot and stayed there. As soon as he did he blocked the lens entirely. I tried to counter as best I could in the small space, hoping the camera could find me. It was not to be, his movements continued to totally block me from the camera. On top of that he turned around with his back to me so that, as written in the scene, my character could write something down using his back as a pad. So now the one person whose opinion was most likely to get me the role or not had his back to me and saw none of my performance for the remainder of the scene. No one else could see me either, nor would they see me when viewing the tape later, as the camera never saw me. Needless to say, I did not get the part, I couldn't possibly get the part. Why would they give it to an invisible actress?

What could I have done? I have racked my brain, believe me, and even in this ridiculous scenario I can think of a few things. I should have found a way, while in character, to simply push the actor into a different position. I was reading for a woman who's a little flaky, and had I ad-libbed something and then taken charge of the blocking it's possible it would have added to their impression of the character. As it was, I could hardly have done anything to make the situation worse, so anything would have been worth a try.

I'm usually pretty good at improvising and being spontaneous and this was the time to use those skills. I believe had I not been influenced by past bad experiences there, and allowed myself to be fully involved with the character, not even his unexpectedly odd movements would have broken my concentration. I would have naturally reacted in a way that had the potential to make the audition work to my advantage. Had I allowed myself to react as the character would have, I may have made a connection with the actor that would have ultimately helped my chances.

This gives me an opportunity to bring up improv. There was nowhere for me to take such classes when I was starting out in New York, but now you can't throw a street pretzel without hitting an improv studio.

Bad Auditions

I think these classes are worth every actor's time, if only for how well they prepare you for auditions. In an improv scene—whether long or short form style—the unexpected is rarely a negative. Having something to respond to while in character is what makes a successful improv move forward. The more the other performers do the more you have to react to.

I think it does wonders for your concentration and spontaneity. Instead of throwing you as a performer, it feeds you, which only increases your focus. In an audition, you have much more "story" to use when the unexpected happens, you've read the script.

At this audition, I could argue that the actor's odd and unpredictable manner should have been a positive, a gift, even, which could have given me an opportunity to deepen my character's qualities on the spot and be more fun for the viewer than a well-presented audition with an off-camera reader would have been. It can be very freeing to play a person who isn't in control, and I was given a great opportunity to delineate that character.

Unfortunately, I didn't recognize it as such.

BAD AUDITION #5

But I Got the Part Anyway

*No longer an ingénue,
take me seriously please.*

BAD AUDITIONS

I had done a Sam Shepard play at a very good regional theatre which was quite well received. A bit later in the season they were casting for their mainstage production of *Three Sisters* and I was asked to read for Irina. This was a different director, and he turned out to be a very nice, very good director, who communicated well. However, I went in knowing I wasn't properly prepared. Irina is one of those roles I *should* have been thrilled to have a chance to do, but somehow it wasn't. I knew deep down that I had never loved the role as much as my fellow ingénues did, and had never longed to play it.

Rather, I had always wanted to play Natasha, a role I had a very strong take on. But on the surface, I reacted as though it was a fabulous opportunity. This game I was playing with myself was dangerous to my process as I half-heartedly prepared for the audition. I was pretending to love the role and be inspired by it, and never addressed my misgivings so I never gave myself the chance to find a way to overcome them and give the best possible performance. At the audition, I felt I did the first scene well but when it came to a more emotional scene I was attempting to portray the emotion without feeling it.

The director said something like "You're so good, why are you holding back?" He said it so simply, so genuinely puzzled, that a little something clicked inside. I suddenly felt foolish, after all why was I faking my way through it? What was such a big deal? What was the point of being there and taking up this nice man's time? We did the scene again and despite my woeful lack of preparation I was able to connect a bit more. I got the role, but it didn't feel like much of a win. I believe it was only because I was physically much as he'd pictured Irina; in addition, he knew the theatre had been pleased with my work earlier that season, and he saw some ability to take direction. I certainly didn't get it because I gave a fabulous audition.

As you might imagine I struggled through rehearsals, feeling the other actors were much more on top of their game, and only during the run did I really feel the connection to Irina that I should have achieved before even auditioning. It was a great learning experience, and important to my overall development to discover how near fatal it can be to let yourself be seen playing a role you haven't taken into your heart.

Despite getting the job, there's plenty of room to reflect on what I could have done differently. Had I fully acknowledged my problem to myself, I could have set about correcting it. There are many tricks an actor possesses and they must be used when one hits a wall emotionally. Tricks such as calling to mind a role that did grab my imagination, and pondering if that feeling could be transferred to help inspire Irina's scenes. When faced with a time crunch, where one is reading for a role with little notice and the magic doesn't happen quickly, it's important to have stored away your own experiences of strong emotional connections, from roles played previously, whether in an acting class or in the professional world.

Those connections never fade, we all have passionate reactions to certain roles. Sometimes calling that

Bad Auditions

to mind can jump start the creative process and help unlock a tangential connection to the problematic role. Staring at Irina's scenes and feeling so blocked was a sign I was desperate to find a way "in" and needed to call on past experience in order to get myself ready, and denying that block was very detrimental.

And the other possibility was to have spent some time working on Natasha's scenes. I didn't have the courage then, but had I asked the director if he'd let me read for her, and articulated my feeling for the role, he may have agreed. It was clear from the start he was flexible and appreciated creative input. And even if he'd said no, I only see you as Irina, he'd have known a bit more about me as an actor, and that could have made his decision easier, rather than the leap of faith he must have taken, to cast someone who gave a mediocre reading. Today I wouldn't hesitate to propose such a thing to a receptive director. I will always wonder if my overall journey might have been different had I developed that courage earlier in my career.

BAD AUDITION #6

Or How I Blew a Self-Tape

Just trying something different.

Bad Auditions

The great thing about self-tape auditions is, or should be, that you have so much more control. You can be sure you like the way you look, and sound, and re-do it until you're happy. I've done many and come to enjoy them; however, I very recently managed to have a Bad Self-Tape Audition.

I was recommended for a role on a high profile, arty TV series, with a Big Fancy Director, who doesn't usually do television. I loved the role and was thrilled to be seen by the BFD. Auditions were held in New York with only the casting people present, but I was in LA and felt a self-tape was preferable, since the creative team wouldn't be in the audition room anyway. The problem was this: I was told about it late one morning and it was due in New York the next day. With the time change I had to do it before the end of the day, or get up extremely early the next day to make the deadline which wasn't a good option. So, I spent the day dividing my time between preparing the sides and setting up the self-tape.

Unfortunately, I hadn't done a self-tape in my LA home in a very long time, and it took quite a while to find the right lighting setup, the right framing, etc. I had just ordered some lamps for this purpose but they hadn't arrived. As a result, I spent as much time with the set-up as on the script. Added to this was that I needed my husband to be my reader, and he was only available for a short time. I wound up being very unhappy with how I looked and my performance. It was just rushed. But I had no choice, I had to upload it at the end of the day.

I had been so busy I neglected to do what should have been my first move: contacting someone I knew in the cast for more information on what they were looking for. When I finally did, he responded the next morning, but by then it was too late. And his information would have been very helpful, as the dialogue was dense and, like many BFD's, this one kept details about the storyline top secret, requiring a lot of guesswork on my part as I quickly crafted my take on the character.

I think it's clear regarding the many things I should have done differently, and there is much to learn about doing self-tapes, which can really be a great tool. Therefore, I'm giving the subject its own chapter, as it seems they are here to stay in our increasingly bi-coastal, and in fact, global, business.

BAD AUDITION #7

The Printer Ate My Sides

Leaning against a weathered doorframe confers gravitas, right?

Bad Auditions

This one is really embarrassing.

I had an audition for a pilot, a very funny role. I wasn't quite right for it, but it was a script with a great pedigree—topnotch writer, producers. I'd be in a room where I wanted to impress. I had three days to prepare, and I was very prepared to knock their socks off. The day before however, I was sent an update, there were script changes. These were long sides, a few different scenes, I had them all memorized and had printed them out of course, I believe it was eleven pages total. The changes weren't very major for my character but there were a number of them. I noticed they were all on three of the pages and rather than print the entire thing out again I just printed the pages that included the new lines. I think some of you, tech-savvy thespians know where this is going already.

I was a bit annoyed, this happens too often, and it makes no sense to me. I realize a pilot is a work in progress, but during the casting process, why incorporate those changes? This doesn't seem like the right venue for the writer/s to find out if the newer jokes are working, and the character is unchanged. Aren't these sessions about finding the right actors? Won't there be at least seven days of rehearsal and shooting and rehearsal for tweaking the script? Anyway, I admit my resentment was behind my decision to just print out the pages that had line changes for me, instead of the whole eleven pages. Not wasting paper was my pathetic act of defiance.

Julia Duffy

The audition room was very friendly, filled with lovely people, welcoming, as conducive as it could be to the performer. I began to do the scene and suddenly was given the wrong line. I was lost, how could this be? I stopped and said but that's not what comes next is it? The reader said oh dear, didn't you get the changes? I said well, yes, but that line wasn't included. She apologized and quickly handed me the page and I saw the line I was supposed to respond to. We started again, got past that part and it happened again. What was she saying? That wasn't in the new or old version. This time she showed me again and once again her page included a line of mine I'd never seen. I was flummoxed and tried to recover, we finished the scenes but of course the comedic rhythm was gone, lost forever.

I was actually in my car before my brain managed to unscramble and analyze the situation—and of course, it was the formatting. The new lines hadn't taken up the same space as the old ones, and by printing out those pages only I'd failed to see that some of the altered dialogue was missing from my poorly collated new sides, which were a hybridized mess of only some of the new dialogue and some of the old.

This was several years ago. I can work a printer now, but even my lousy tech skills weren't to blame here. Only I was to blame. I let my annoyance—okay, my pissiness—alter my preparation. I had the scene so well memorized and thought out, when the changes were sent, I resented having to make an adjustment for something so unnecessary. I didn't carefully read the new sides and on top of that I failed to notice that a couple of lines of dialogue no longer tracked. I was so attached to my original take on the material that I rushed through reading and memorizing my few new lines.

And to make it even worse, I didn't take responsibility. I was so sure it was their fault I allowed those in the room to keep apologizing for what they felt must have been their screw-up. I should have instantly taken responsibility even without feeling sure, in my confusion, I'd done anything wrong. It would have been best, by far, to say, *hey, I think I must have gotten something wrong here and I'm a bit lost, let me step out for a few minutes and come back in.* I can't imagine they would have said no, especially if I'd done it as soon as it occurred, rather than after my befuddlement no doubt caused them to dismiss me as a serious candidate for the role.

I recently had an audition where I believe the above painful lesson benefited me. I was reading for the role of a teacher, very funny, very in control of her class—a no nonsense type. As I began to do the scene I was perhaps a bit too pumped up and said a wrong word in the first line. I caught myself—in a nanosecond I realized I'd noticed it, therefore my focus had been momentarily lost, and it was going to affect my performance. I couldn't afford to lose focus for even a beat because it would affect the comic rhythms. Almost without thinking I said, in my best teacher voice: "Hold on—I'm starting over." They quickly said oh, okay, and I relaunched into it. I knew I had to do it quickly, before they had formed too much an impression—all those times I failed to rescue a sinking audition paid off now, they were very responsive. It helped that I was playing someone who was pretty dominant, that's true, announcing I was starting over worked within the character. But it also helped that I'd been there, done that, and learned from it.

The Waiting Room

I'm done smiling in pictures, enough already.

Bad Auditions

I grew up Catholic and there was much talk of Purgatory in my religious education. We used to say ejaculations [yes, that is the word] while waiting in the lunch line. Each ejaculation [Jesus, Mary, and Joseph, for example], was listed in some sort of holy card dispensed to us, with the number of days it would reduce one's time in Purgatory. Of course, we all figured we could get away with a fair number of sins if we just did enough . . . ejaculating. We tried to do the math, if I lie to my mother how many ejaculations should I say to shorten that part of my sentence in the afterlife? Little did I know I wouldn't have to wait until the afterlife to experience Purgatory, because I became an actress and therefore the waiting room would be my Purgatory.

Let me hasten to say I have met some wonderful actresses in the waiting room. I call them waiting room relationships, because we rarely if ever work together. The odds of two women the same age in any one script are low, that is the reality of women's roles, especially in TV and film. Most of them are generous, professional, and bring good humor to our shared situation, and it does create a bond. Having said that, it still feels like Purgatory. There is nothing at all conducive about sitting and making small talk, or sitting in awkward silence, with your competition.

For starters, I often walk in surprised by who's sitting there. It can alter your perception of the role to see who else is being considered. I've been much younger, always much shorter, often less pretty, sometimes much older, both much better and much lesser known than my fellow waiters. It's a great deal of information to process upon entering, when the only thing in my head should be the character I'm about to play. Add to that the all too common situation of being able to hear what's happening in the audition room, and it's too much to hope one can remain in the hard-won bubble of concentration achieved from intense preparation.

My advice is obvious: get the hell out of Purgatory. If you have to alert a harried assistant that you'll be outside the door or down the hall out of earshot, do so. It's your right to do what's required to be professional. I've also taken to bringing my earbuds to block out sound, play conducive music, and it keeps others from chatting with me if I am forced to stay in the room.

There is one small advantage to being in the waiting room, though. Often you can catch a glimpse of the audition room. There isn't a great deal of variety in how audition rooms are set up, but I personally find it helpful to see how large it is, how the furniture is arranged, and where the reader is posted. I'm sure not everyone has such a literal visual sense as me, but I still envision whether I'm looking right or left of camera, whether they're sitting or standing and so on. I don't even realize how strongly this has affected my imagination until I walk in and discover something quite different. Just recently I walked into one room that was surprisingly large, and I admit I was thrown by how far away I had to stand from the camera and the reader. It was much farther away than the two people in the scene would be from each other. So: take a peek, if you can.

And now it's time to discuss just that—the audition room itself.

In The Room

*Headshot fatigue quite evident
in my expression.*

Bad Auditions

So, you've prepared, you're beautifully memorized, you had just the right outfit in your closet and now you enter the room. A sample of what the room's occupants opening remarks might be:

- *Hi Julia, nice to see you again* [now you know you've met before, but casting people never realize how little the actor remembers faces from an audition room.]
- *Julia! We're such fans, so glad you're here! Loved your work on _____.*[something recently aired.]
- *Hi. You are??* [state your name]
- *Stand on the tape mark please.*
- *State your name and height* [feel free to lie about the second one if that's best. There are no height police.]
- *Do you have any questions?* [This one always throws me, because yes, I usually have one but forgot it.]
- *Just ignore the stage directions, we're really not looking for her to be that crazy/hysterical/nasty/silly/dumb.*
- *We aren't going with an accent after all.*
- *Don't play her drunk, that's been cut.*
- *We're just going to do the second scene* [or whatever scene has the least character beats/emotion in it.]
- *Did you get the new pages?*

63

Julia Duffy

Ok, this is why in my bad audition stories you'll find I refer to rehearsing it different ways when prepping. It's hard to do it differently from the way you feel strongest about, it's like ignoring an impulse. But it can truly help if you've spent at least a bit of time trying something else at home, because you will be less thrown when something unexpected occurs in the room. And you never know what you might find in the character by trying something else.

I was once told not to play it drunk, just before going in to read for the network honchos. This being a character who was always drunk in the script. I don't know when they decided to change it, but they decided to tell *me* just as I went in for the final callback.

I have a few bits of advice here. Advice as to how to handle these things is tricky, because any strong choice can backfire. It's the risk in making such a choice, and if asked you didn't hear these things from me, I'll deny it.

If a big change is thrown at you, you can ask to go out and have a few minutes before continuing. Asking that feels huge, I know, but remember, you're there to do a job, and you want to do it well. Give yourself that opportunity. At least as far as asking for a moment to digest a note, don't be afraid to do so. There will be many times on a set, or in rehearsal, that you will need to pause and gather yourself emotionally while people are watching. It's helpful to find ways to get used to that. It should not be weird, it's part of this art form, always has been, always will be. They often start the camera and say "whenever you're ready." They mean it, they want to see your best. Take, and *use*, your moment.

One way to make a room feel warmer is if you

walk in and introduce yourself, with all your enthusiasm for being there on display. People like you to be excited about their project. Sometimes waiting for them to speak first takes a bit of your power over your audience away.

If a last-minute adjustment is thrown at you say something like "Okay, great, let me try that." If you feel it was impossible to make the adjustment all at once try something along the lines of "I love that note/adjustment/idea. Can I try it once more? It's so different from how I prepared it."

Anytime you ask for something in the audition room, whether it's to do it sitting, or for the reader to sit or stand, or to do it again—anything—ask it with enthusiasm. Avoid sounding needy. I've asked for many things, and I learned after a while that they almost always said *yes* when it was presented in the spirit of "ooh, ooh, I love this, can I try this?" [Don't say *ooh ooh* though.] Note the difference between meekly asking permission to do something and being afraid the answer will be no, and asking permission to do something because you're enthusiastic about how much it will make this joint effort better. YOU are helping THEM cast this role, and you are happy to do so.

The last thing I want to touch on regarding the room is staying in character. Mostly I think you should. Nothing wrong with them seeing your process. You might notice that when doing a scene, in a class or rehearsal, you listen to the director, or teacher, and take it all in while focusing on the scene you're doing. You might be listening with your eyes closed, or looking at the floor or off into space as you process the input. In a rehearsal situation, this is expected. You are not being rude or unsociable, you're just keeping your concentration going while being directed, or critiqued.

An audition is a similar creative situation, except that it begins with introductions and niceties. You will have to be more sociable than you would be in class or rehearsal. But not that much more. Realize what the dynamic is between the two forces and get comfortable with it. It's okay if you seem a bit distracted and intense while greeting them and exchanging information. Intensity and enthusiasm are the same things, products of your hard work and commitment to the role. As long as your focus is on making sure they see your take on the role none of your choices will be wrong.

Lastly, I personally detest slating on camera before beginning the scene. Whether in the room or when doing a self-tape, I no longer look into the camera to announce my name. I have my eyes where they will be for the start of the scene [usually just off-camera, looking at my reader], and quickly say my name, then I take a moment. They just need your name, it doesn't matter how you say it. Just don't let the slate get in the way of your initial attack on the scene.

And I have a word of advice when it's a Good Audtion, and you receive praise. Do not dwell on the compliment and if possible use the moment to reinforce your feeling for the role. Saying something like "Well this material is so inspiring", or "It's just so funny on the page" can go a long way, especially if the writer is in the room. In other words, take all praise and criticism as being about the work, not about you as a person.

Oh Crap, They Want A Monologue

Bad Auditions

I don't have any Bad Audition stories about monologue auditions, perhaps because I've blocked them all out. I groaned whenever I was told to have a monologue prepared, and I honestly don't know how often young actors are asked to do one these days, but I do know they are an inescapable part of getting into theatre schools and programs. So I am assuming there's still a need for some advice, especially as the number of monologue books out there seem to have multiplied greatly.

Personally, I grew weary of trying to decide which monologue to do whenever I was told "They have sides but want you to have a monologue ready." I had several at the ready but I began to question how effective they really were, and it wasn't a good sign that the thought of doing them made me groan. I decided to take some time and try to find one that I really liked, and I wound up getting very lucky.

I only now realize how lucky I was, as in recent years I've informally coached some students, usually for college auditions. I saw how common the earnest, staring straight out with feet planted, very sad or very angry monologue has become. They are the most prevalent, the easiest to find. And I'm sure some actors make a great impression with this type, but I can imagine what it's like for the person watching monologue auditions all day, and having one that departs a bit from the usual fare can possibly shake them awake.

69

Julia Duffy

My search led me to the Lincoln Center Library, my usual haunt. I found a reference book of monologues, something that wasn't common then. Each one in the list had the first line of the monologue in it. The one that caught my eye had the opening line "This is my father." I thought that was a rather intriguing start, and they did have the play, an obscure British play called *The Party* by Jane Arden. I took it home and fell in love with it, went back, took out all the other copies they had and never returned them. I'm not technically a felon though, I paid the entire fine for five lost books. So basically I bought the exclusive U.S rights to my monologue since it wasn't available anywhere else.

The speech occurs at the end of the play, and it involves the character—a teenage girl—realizing her father is about to leave. She stops him and desperately tries to make up for all that's gone wrong between them, by pretending they're at the party she had forbidden him to attend. As she tries to show how it all should have gone, she goes around the room attempting to create it, turning down the lights, decorating, etc. She introduces him to her invisible friends and tells them about him, trying to create the party she'd wanted but sabotaged. At the end she can't continue, she just dissolves into sorrow.

The reason this monologue is so ideal is that it required urgency, movement, with stakes very high for the character. Most importantly, it was directed AT someone, not out towards the void. Looking at an empty chair and pretending it contained an actor wasn't necessary, she's too flustered and busy to look directly at him for very long.

The other great advantage is that without knowing the story, it was very apparent to the viewer what was going on. Setting up the scene or knowing the play wasn't necessary to draw the viewer into the story. It solved all my monologue problems, and I did it many times. And even several years later there were people I ran across again who recalled seeing me do it. I'll take some credit, but the fact that it was beautifully and powerfully written, and intrigued those watching and made them want to know more about the play was an enormous advantage.

Besides my powerful emotional connection to it, the movement, punctuated by sudden stillness as the character deflates after her desperate effort, gave me an opportunity to show multiple and even conflicting feelings simultaneously. I urge you, at a time when you DON'T have an audition looming, to search out a monologue that plays to your strengths, and captivates you.

And I should add I'm personally against monologues from books that aren't from a play. For one thing, my teachers would have been appalled if I'd brought in such a thing to work on. There is a great advantage to knowing the whole arc of a character, from a published play that has been audience-tested. If you love the character and the monologue, you will no doubt love the other scenes that showcase him or her. In addition, with all that background material you are more likely to embody the character and bring a distinct and fully fleshed person to life in the audition room.

Being creative and passionate about your choice will pay off. I was coaching a very talented young actress a few years ago and she did her monologues for me. All were great. For one of her auditions, the theater program had a callback situation for those who made the first cut, and asked them to bring in something

Julia Duffy

additional next time, preferably a role that wasn't obviously right for them. She said to me "just because it's a monologue, does it have to be only talking? I have two of those already, can it be mostly silent?" I was stunned by this idea. I said I don't know, what are you thinking? She said she wanted to do the scene from *Flowers for Algernon* where Charley is no longer on the drug and is sliding back to being mentally challenged, inarticulate Charley, and is reacting to feeling his limitations again. He's alone and getting increasingly anguished as he attempts a simple task, saying little but of course moaning, and grunting, building up to a breakdown.

She did it for me and it was amazing. I said, yeah, you must do it. She got into a very good school. So get creative. When you find your killer monologue, you can't miss.

DEALING WITH FRUSTRATION,

OR WHY DIDN'T I GET THE PART?

BAD AUDITIONS

Let's take a side trip here to Good Audition Land, and the frustration of doing well and not being rewarded. I have had this happen, and so will you because life is apparently not fair, a concept I still can't get used to. The concept itself is just so unfair.

Here is one example from my Good Audition but no job experience—actually several—as a series of auditions at NBC became my own real life mini-series. The head of casting for years was a guy I'll call Joel Thurm, because that's his name. This was in the era of networks competing to have the biggest, priciest, most dramatic and award-worthy TV movies and miniseries each season. For a period of time that seems like decades in my memory (but may have been only a year or two), I was constantly going to the network to audition for these epics.

Sometimes there were many girls waiting to read, sometimes only a few, occasionally it was a final audition narrowed down to myself and one other. Time after time I lost out, but I kept getting sent to the network callbacks. Many of these roles were young women who suffered greatly and met bad ends, often they were cast with actresses who very much specialized in suffering. Sometimes I lost out because they really wanted a girl who was stunning to look at, sometimes they wanted someone more plain. Joel began to tease when he saw me. "I see you're here for the ugly role" he said when I sat waiting with no makeup on, looking teary.

Then came the one I thought I'd finally land, despite knowing the girl was written to be especially stunning. But the role was complex, beauty alone could not carry it. I kept getting called back, in one session they even made me up and did some Polaroids of me in various attire, trying to make me more glamorous. Each audition went well, I was deeply connected to the role. In the end, of course beauty won out, a far more glamorous actress got the part. And though she went on to a big career she was not well received in this role, she was young and inexperienced and beauty wasn't enough.

A few weeks after it aired I was guesting on another NBC show and Joel came by the set. We were standing to the side during a rehearsal, chatting, and he suddenly mentioned the TV movie. He said "we should have cast you, we'd have had a better movie. There, I said it." Then he quickly walked away.

My first reaction was to feel the sorrow over losing that role again, it was like it had happened to me a second time. But eventually I let myself be flattered and comforted. One rarely gets to hear what the casting powers really think, and they're right to keep their comments in reserve regarding the producer's final choices. I was given a gift by him, it was useful to have an idea of just how much my work was valued during that arduous audition process.

And this is what I'm hoping to convey here—that auditioning is part of your body of work, especially when you're starting out, even auditions that you aren't likely to get are helping to build your reputation, and define the qualities people will associate with you. Each audition is about more than that job. And it's not just what the casting powers will learn about you, but what YOU will learn about yourself as well. Your recognition of how you fit into the scheme of things, how your singular vision of a role makes you an interesting choice, that will give it a quality specific to you, these are things only auditions can teach you. They may cast someone else, but they'll know they can't get YOUR x-factor. It's a win if you've made it a tough choice for them.

And the funny thing about my story is that with the perspective I have now, I know the casting had to go that way. Of course they would only cast someone as beautiful as the script required. It wasn't a shallow indulgence, it was integral to the story, and this girl absolutely had the beauty and overall quality it called for. Me, I was cute. As much as I treasure what Joel said to me later, he was probably wrong, the nature of the project would have been quite changed by casting me. Most of the time the right thing happens in the casting world. It may break your heart, but there are so many factors involved, all the stars have to align for you to get the role, and how well you audition is just one of those stars.

The next time I saw Joel it was also for a role I didn't get. I was wrong for it in some way I can't remember now, and knew I was. He kind of laughed when he saw me, knowing I wouldn't get this one either. He walked over to me and handed me something. It was a lifetime parking pass for NBC Studios. He figured I'd be back.

Self-Tape Auditions

You Should Still Get Nervous

Bad Auditions

Self-tape auditions take practice. They can't be rushed, or done casually. They must capture attention from the first moment. It's common to do a take, look at it, and be appalled at how low energy it feels. If you've experienced this it's no doubt because the frisson of energy provided by nerves in an audition room is absent. You have no audience. My personal solution to this is to do it repeatedly, I find that each time I become more precise, trying to achieve perfection, having viewed the previous takes and seeing the flaws. The fact that you have the *chance* to achieve perfection should get your juices flowing. You have no distractions, no one is reacting, you don't have to process outside stimuli while doing the scene, it's exciting to have the opportunity to find the fullest performance possible.

You can become your own demanding director, insisting on getting that great moment from Take Two and that other one from Take Four in the same take as the powerful delivery you achieved in Take Six. Maybe Take Seven will be the one. I once spent hours on a self-tape for a theatre role, until finally I felt I'd gotten all I wanted into one take. I uploaded it and went to bed. The next day I woke up and had a new idea, and did it all over again, several times, took down the one I'd uploaded, and replaced it with the new take. I got the part.

The lesson here is: don't take down your set-up too quickly. Your brain will keep working. So instead of getting that bit of inspiration while driving home from the audition and kicking yourself for not thinking of it earlier, you just may have it in time to do something about it. So let yourself get nervous, and obsessive, as you shoot your close-up and have this opportunity to send your best to be viewed by Important People.

And this takes time. You need the following components to do your best:

- A room that has decent acoustics, you want to avoid a hollow sound. Or order a mic that can attach to your device and clip on your clothing.
- A blank space behind you, ideally hang a sheet or curtain that's a good backdrop color like blue.
- A decent camera, which of course most devices have now. I use an iPad Mini.
- A clamp for said device is highly recommended. There are many available, some are quite lightweight so you can travel with it should you not be home when a self-tape opportunity arises. Clamps are very helpful in that you can adjust the angle of the camera that best suits your face.
- Lighting. I know people who have professional light kits, on stands or tabletop ones. I have three cylinder lamps from Home Depot that cost $20.00 each and I use LED bulbs in them. I get the effect I want without it looking fancy. If you want your eyes to "pop," it's important to have the light get in there. Depending on whether I'm sitting or standing, or moving my head a lot, I may use things, like books, to raise the iPad and or the lights.
- A reader. Preferably someone patient. Even better if it's someone who owes you a favor and you

won't have to feel self-conscious about how long you make them sit there and read the scene with you.

Here I insert a disclaimer: there might be casting people who would argue with some of the things I'm telling you. I've taken it upon myself to give advice because I've done quite a few, and have been cast three times directly from self-tapes, including a theatre job. I've occasionally been given instruction from the casting office on what they want on the tape, and it doesn't vary much. A plain background, no costuming or props [though I might put a pair of glasses on and off, or drink from a glass as part of the scene. I seem to audition for a lot of drunks.] They often want you to slate, which I do in character, I do NOT look into the camera when doing so, I want the entire viewing experience to be watching a scene, period.

From all I've heard casting people say they do not want a "produced" tape. Think about what the tape from the casting session looks like. A blank wall, less than lovely lighting, perhaps a full body shot before they zoom in and then I'm quite sure they stay in medium close-up for the bulk of the scene. 99% of my self-tapes are done because I'm not able to be at the in-person casting session. So, my tape will be downloaded along with the ones filmed in the room. It's best if it isn't jarringly different.

You do, however, want it to "pop." The Important People viewing it are looking at many in a row, hopefully on a state-of-the-art high resolution monitor. But they could also be looking at an iPad while eating lunch at their desk. Your look should be somehow emphatic, so even if you're playing a drab sort of individual don't fade into the background. Don't wear beige in front of a beige wall.

And if you're doing a self-tape for theatre my best advice is find some moment where your body language is conveyed. On stage, as you know, the tension, your physical bearing, are a large part of your performance. Your opportunity to show that in a self-tape is limited of course, but if the scene allows for it I try to find a section where I'm back from the camera for a bit. But of course, it's a camera, it's going to be viewed on a screen, you will almost certainly need to reveal yourself in a medium close-up for maximum impact.

My most urgent piece of advice is obvious after reading Bad Audition #6—be prepared in advance. Find the lighting, the room, the angle, that works best in your house, or wherever you choose to do these. Film yourself in various looks and learn what works best. I would even suggest uploading some of these "tests" to whatever site you use, because the video quality has a tendency to look different, as well as the framing format, than it looks when played back on your device. If you spend some time testing the result you get with the tools you have you'll be ready when the next self-tape arises, and you can spend your time as an actor, preparing the scene. It is very distracting to also be a cinematographer while preparing an audition.

And there is one more reason to "practice" self-tapes in advance of needing to do one. You can do this when preparing for an in-person audition before you go. Who knows, it could help you walk into that room with a more polished performance.

My Best Audition

or What a Difference the Casting Person Can Make

Bad Auditions

I arrived in Hollywood in the late seventies, fresh from a Broadway play, which was like arriving in Hollywood *not* having done a Broadway play. They are simply two different worlds, and though the west coast does influence show business on the east coast, influence in that regard does not travel against the prevailing winds. There is little about having done stage that translates into a concrete reason to cast someone in an on-camera role. It's a simple truth, no point in dwelling on it. There really are several businesses within our business.

As an ingénue, one gets quickly determined to be either comedic or dramatic. So, within a few weeks of auditioning half the LA casting people thought of me as a dramatic actress, the other half a comedic one, depending on what role I first auditioned for in their room. And I almost as quickly noticed that I had an edge with comedy. With dramatic roles, I often found myself competing with great beauties, who had knockout figures, and since the ingénue is frequently the object of romance, the visual was primary. However, if you could make them laugh it mattered far less if you physically embodied their vision. I continued going up for dramatic roles for quite some time, but it was in the auditions for comedic roles that I found my courage. And there was one casting person who never, ever, saw me as just one or the other: Fran Bascom, casting director at MTM.

I had an audition for *Lou Grant*, one of the most critically acclaimed shows at that time. I was thrilled to go up for something so prestigious. In those days, there were no computers so one had a choice: go to the audition early and spend time with the sides, or drive over the day before and pick them up. Luckily, I drove over the day before and in this case, they were handing out the whole script.

My heart sank when I saw the role, however. A nurse in the waiting area of the emergency room. The most scintillating line was "I'm afraid there will be a wait to see the doctor." How could I possibly impress this important casting office with a role like that? But I had time so I read the whole script. I went into high alert when I got to a scene in which the investigative reporter stops in a fast food place to ask questions of a teenager working at the counter. It was extremely short, and she had no useful information. Having seen the show, I knew how quirky and humorous they sometimes made these scenes and I thought this had that potential.

I decided to make an attempt to also read for that role.

The next day I dressed conservatively as one would to play a nurse, but I brought with me a change of clothes and some clips for my hair. I read for the nurse, and felt just as flat as I feared, and then said to Ms. Bascom, "You know I feel so much more right for the counter girl in that other scene, so I've prepared it. Could I change my look and read for that?" She said "Yes, go out and come back and I'll bring you in."

I did. I quickly changed, added some makeup and a new hairdo and put gum in my mouth. She had me in and I proceeded to show her my take on the role,

Bad Auditions

that this girl was every reporter's nightmare, abrupt, bored, totally disinterested in answering his questions. She loved the idea and said she was taking me over to the producers [this was common at that time, auditions weren't taped to be viewed later.]

I still had to read for the nurse when I got to the producer's room, but in the elevator going up there my co-conspirator Fran said "Okay, after you read, go change and I'll get you back in." After reading for the nurse I once again changed into the gum-chewing teenager and returned. She walked me into the room and said "Okay, I just want Julia to do this other scene for you."

They laughed, I got the part, and that tiny role paved the way for the casting powers at MTM to see me as a comedic actress, which eventually led to an audition for *Newhart* a few years later which of course was life-changing. Well, I should say, *most* of the casting powers at MTM then considered me a comedic actress. Fran just thought of me as an actress, and continued to have me in for a variety of roles. She even brought me in once for a trailer-trash, boozing, abusive mother. Everyone in the waiting room looked the type, and when I asked why she brought me in she said "Oh, I know you can do it. It will be interesting, and they need to expand their view of the role." They did not wind up doing so, but she made sure they had the opportunity.

I saw Fran occasionally over the years, the last time was about six years ago, I was doing *The Heiress* at the Pasadena Playhouse, playing Aunt Lavinia. She came backstage, had loved the play and said it didn't surprise her to see me in this dramatic character role. She immediately brought up the *Lou Grant* audition. I

Julia Duffy

had the great good fortune to be able to tell her, some thirty-plus years later, how much that meant to me. I hope I articulated it properly to her, that she saw me, really saw ME, and that respect endowed me with courage. Her attitude was "Oh, you would have made it in this business regardless."

Well, maybe... maybe so. But the confidence she gave me sure helped.

DEAR TWENTY-YEAR OLD ME

Regrets And Wisdom, Mostly Wisdom

Bad Auditions

Regrets. I've had a few.

I wonder if all actors feel it took them way too long to reach their potential. Except I'm not sure any of us ever do. I'm a better actress now than I was in my twenties, than I was in my forties, than I was last week. Because the learning, the evolving, never stop. I do know some fabulously talented actors who will tell you they are horrible at auditions, yet somehow, they had great careers. This book isn't for them.

Let's get the regrets over with first. You've read some of the specific ones, but here are general ones that I truly would correct if I were to do it over. I would have wasted less of my money on singing lessons. Not just because I'm not a singer, and they were a big help in making me able to use my voice to the best of it's potential. I lost any fear of singing and it's amazing how many times I've needed to sing in a role. Not well, but for one reason or another I played someone who sang—either badly for comedic effect, because it was a Christmas scene and there was caroling, once I was a mom singing to her baby, etc.

So, I'm glad I spent some effort in trying to sing, but seriously, twenty-year-old me, that was never your future. What were you thinking? My resources weren't infinite and I should have invested in other classes after I finished school. I could have brought some of my problems into class, expressed my concerns about various epic audition fails, and used the class to bolster the confidence needed to nail more of those chances.

I also should have sought out individual coaching, especially when I had an audition for something major. I had great opportunities that not everyone gets and I could have done more to make them count. I became rather independent, a self-starter, which is a good thing and a bad thing. One often has to be, you don't get a brilliant director every time, or the best material, or the most ideal scene partner. But I do think I needed to shake things up, bring another dynamic into my work, and living in New York I had access to many kinds of teachers and coaches. Even just an occasional expenditure on a coach before a challenging audition could have done much to push my development forward, beyond that particular audition.

One of the most tangible things that could have come out of taking more classes after I left school is that I could have worked on roles in which I normally didn't get cast. I needed to expand my own vision of my "type" and what I was capable of. I was attracted to offbeat, dark roles, but I looked the typical ingénue and it was many years before I could figure out how to make that dichotomy work to my advantage. I was always far too aware of what I thought I was and wasn't right for, and that persists today. If I'd been able to let go of my own preconceived notions of my "type," I feel it would have led to others expanding their vision of me.

And I could have used my fellow actors—friends perhaps—to practice the audition, whenever there was enough time to arrange that. Or, something that never occurred to me—older actors with whom I'd worked. One should use all resources available to make the most of a great opportunity. What I know now, and can assure younger actors, is that veteran actors are quite willing to help. It's very common to feel almost

BAD AUDITIONS

a sense of mission in passing along acquired wisdom, and I imagine that feeling exists in veterans of many professions outside of acting. In point of fact, this author felt something akin to an obligation to write a book sharing the very things that would have been welcome information when I was starting out.

Inspiration can come from other sources too. Reading biographies of accomplished people of all creative disciplines can be very formative. This is something I did do a lot, and I can still remember how profoundly some resonated with me. What I did not do was expand my horizons by becoming familiar with various styles, for want of another word, of acting.

Here's an example: I had an audition for a new play, being produced in a venue I now forget, but still recall it being a place where I really wanted to work, and with a director I'd kill to work for. I was dead right for the role; it was very much my kind of comedy. However, the play had a very unique style, as it encompassed the hallmarks of bygone styles, especially old American movies.

Later in my twenties I became fanatical about old films, but at this time I was fairly unexposed to that style. In particular the speaking pattern of so many old movie stars, that mid-Atlantic accent that was so popular in the thirties and forties. It did not matter how funny I felt I could be in the role, it absolutely required an ability to mimic that style. There was no crash course possible, this was even before VCRs. All I could do was check the listings to see if any old movies that fit this genre were airing in the next couple of days. There were none. What I'm saying here is: expand your horizons. Be curious about culture and style from past decades, past centuries. If something was big once, if it was "a thing," it probably influenced current culture in some way. A script may have a line where a character imitates Walter Brennan. You don't want to have to ask who Walter Brennan was. [If you are now asking that: cowboy movies.]

Now it's much easier, now there is truly no excuse to be unfamiliar with any reference needed to understand a script or character. And as for accents—yes, young me, you should have taken on that learning curve much earlier, *before* you needed it. Of course at that time, a dialect coach or purchasing a set of teaching tapes were my only options. I know now that even one session with a dialect coach can be a huge help with mastering an accent. And of course these days you can learn anything online, for free. My husband recently learned to ride a horse online. Yes, you read that correctly. He was asked to do a role in a very cool webseries about a Civil War battle. So, horses. He watched some lessons on YouTube and did quite well. Didn't break anything.

Back to accents. I definitely lost some roles because I had no time to master one. Whatever we worked on in school hadn't stayed with me. I suggest working on whatever accent/s are likely to come up repeatedly for you. If you're a New York type, work on that one. I can attest that Southern comes up a lot, both rural and refined. I suppose British is still a good one to have, though I'm not sure, since these days they seem to have a readily available pool of actual Brit actors in both New York and L.A. It is amazing how many are here, or get hired from across the pond by self-tapes. But don't get me started.

This is the nuts and bolts wisdom, knowing now what I should have been doing in general, in my down

BAD AUDITIONS

time, of which I had plenty. Then there's the wisdom about yourself, that comes from the hard-won courage gained from going forward after failure. After the 100th audition [hopefully sooner] or so, you get wise to yourself. You know if you were good, you know if you could have done better. If you don't feel those things, then you aren't paying attention. Your gut isn't wrong, your gut is there for a reason, listen to it. If you trust your gut, you'll find your courage. And it's the courage that brings you the flexibility, the spontaneity that is needed in auditions, and in the work process itself.

You may get a note at an audition to do something else, and in your gut, you feel it's wrong. This is where flexibility is crucial. A great exercise in an acting class, or a how-to-audition class, would be to prepare a scene, and have the teacher throw adjustments at you. Finding how to comply with that and still maintain the strength of your performance is the key to success, it's the key to making those five minutes in the room really count.

I have been humbled many times by the following scenario: I'm rehearsing a scene, or perhaps shooting it, and the director gives me a note that feels odd. I resist, it's not at all what I feel emotionally. After some back and forth I try it. Maybe do it a few more times, maybe—if I'm rehearsing a play—I continue trying that adjustment for the next few days, each time we run that scene. Suddenly I see what the director meant, and I feel something new and valid and my notion of the scene is deepened exponentially.

All from a note I first resisted. I wonder why I didn't see it before. I needed to both trust my gut, and retain my openness, a tricky balance. Because, here's the thing—*you will never stop auditioning.* Even if you become established, and roles are offered to you, the first read-thru, the first take you film of your first scene on your first day on set, the first time you try an adjustment after being given a note by the director in front of everyone—they are *all* auditions. All require courage, all take place in a high-stakes environment, in every one of those situations you are once again presenting your work for judgment and need to be at your best. Learning how to focus under pressure and commit quickly to a suggestion are skills needed all through an actor's career. And auditions will be your best teachers.

Learn from every single time you act—from your auditions, your classes, your own solitary work at home, your self-tapes that you can view and try to better each time. The more you learn about yourself the more you will start to love auditions, and you MUST learn to love them, they are the most important aspect of your career, of your art form. I suggest learning from the "yes—and" model in improv: Yes, I can do it that way, Yes it would be fun to try it with/without the accent, Yes, I'll grab this opportunity to shove the actor out of the way so he's not blocking me. Yes, I'm ready to do this. Yes, I understand this specific style. Yes, I will show you everything I have inside me. Yes, I'm nervous but it doesn't matter because I'm also deeply connected to this character. Yes, I can do it angrily even though it says sweetly. Yes, I do need a moment to adjust/focus. Yes, I bobbled that line but I'm on fire here, so just hold on a moment. Yes, I can do it better next time, and the next. Yes. Yes. Yes.

Epilogue

Bad Auditions

I began this book with a bad audition, and followed with more humiliating stories, but now I'd like to end with a good one. It illustrates just how delicate this audition business is, how the smallest thing can affect how it goes in that room.

I wanted to audition for the play *The Little Foxes* at the Pasadena Playhouse. I knew no one would ever think of me for the role of Birdie, but I decided to work on it just in case I got an appointment. My manager started pushing them to see me three months beforehand, but the response was polite and noncommittal. I figured it was a good exercise even if I didn't get the audition, so I began to work on the role. When they finally called with an appointment I had less than twenty-four hours' notice, so I was very glad I'd spent all that time on it and had it memorized.

The stakes are very high when you've pushed someone to let you audition and raised their expectations, so I was quite nervous, and I feared that the casting director, Michael Donovan, was risking having his usually excellent judgment questioned by bringing me in. And so I was feeling a bit of extra pressure. As I was leaving the house, my daughter, also an actress, called. I told her I was on my way to an important audition. She said don't forget to have fun. I laughed and said well, it's for an abused alcoholic. She said you'll be acting, you still have to have fun. As I drove there, trying to calm my nerves, I thought about her words. And I thought well, is it *fun*? Is that why I've loved this role so much? I thought about the part of the scene I most looked forward to doing, and how I knew I couldn't miss, that when I got to that moment I would be having fun. I couldn't wait for that moment. And when it arrived, I did. I had fun. It was dramatic and tragic and challenging, and I had fun. I got the part.

Acknowledgments

Bad Auditions

By now some readers might be thinking fine, thanks for sharing, but how the hell can I use your advice if I can't get auditions in the first place? I realize that advice on how to be your best self in "the room" is useless if one can't get *into* the room. I know how hard it is to get representation today, much more difficult than it was when I started. My school—The American Academy of Dramatic Arts—had long-standing relationships with agents around New York City. Many of them attended our senior productions, and I benefited from this exposure, as I looked so young I was always cast in age-appropriate roles, so I was seen doing exactly the kind of roles an agent would submit me for.

I was very lucky, and I know it. Now a theater student hopes to get exposure through senior showcases, and though agents dutifully attend these, they need to judge an actor's potential on rather brief stage time. The world of show business as I knew it has changed dramatically. This of course is due to the internet. It both gives opportunity and reduces it. It has made breaking into show business something anyone can get information about. Prior to this vast resource being available only the most determined and obsessed young people found their way into casting offices. Now there are hordes of would-be actors majoring in theater at hundreds of colleges and universities offering these programs, or arriving in New York and Los Angeles to begin the process of finding decent representation. The sheer numbers are staggering.

At the same time the internet has made it possible to make something and show it to an audience, an opportunity I'd have given my eye teeth for. Waiting for a chance to act was torture for me, there was little I or anyone could do but wait for someone to produce something and then hope to audition for it. There were very few ways to inexpensively showcase yourself. I envied artists, they could pick up a paintbrush and make art. My fellow actors and I needed much more to practice our intangible art form. Now there is the opportunity to make your own art, and a place to post it for all to see.

Advice on how to get in the room, how to get representation, and be seen by casting people is of course a subject for another book, and there are many of them. I am fully aware that it is the hardest part of this profession, but I do believe any actor who has real talent will, despite the numerical odds, eventually find his or her way into The Room if a determined and unflagging effort is mounted. And though I had a great deal of luck I am able to pass on some excellent advice on getting ahead in today's business, from some smart actors I know who have gotten themselves into The Room without luck or advantages. Here is a summary of what I've learned from them:

- If you're hoping to audition for guest roles, a category that tends to have the most job openings, watch TV, especially shows that shoot in the town where you live. It's good to be aware of what shows cast actors like yourself, and what shows you feel strongly about. You'll be better prepared to audition for a show if you fully grasp its particular tone. Don't try to wing it. Never try to wing an audition, knowledge is power.

Bad Auditions

- If you decide to take casting director workshops keep in mind you should choose ones taught by official casting directors, who are in charge of casting TV, film, commercials, and theater. There are some questionable ones who "charge" for auditions. This is not kosher. But a legitimate casting director becoming familiar with your work can be a very positive step and I know a number of actors who have gotten called in for auditions by the person they took the workshop with. Just be sure you check their bio.

- I love this advice a casting director gave to my friend Ruth: "Don't go into an audition trying to do what you think the producer is looking for. Do the role as it would be with RUTH playing it. If you're wrong for it they still will have seen what you do well, what your quality is, and next time you'll be called in for something you fit well."

Never be afraid to sell yourself. You're selling your talent, it's a commodity, it is needed, and you have every right to find a way to do what you've trained for. You have every right to boldly try to get into The Room, where you also have a right to have your best efforts succeed or fail, it is the only way for either to take place so your talent can be honed. This book with it's deliberate title is intended to help you fulfill your destiny, and learning from setbacks—mine and yours—is a crucial part of that.

In closing I'd like to thank my family, for general support and encouragement, and listening to my Bad Audition stories on those difficult days. Others have encouraged me regarding this book as well, most notably Mary Lou Belli, a director and author of books for both

107

actors and directors. Finally I wish to thank all those casting people I've met in The Room over the years, the ones who made it hard and the ones who made it a delight. I learned from both kinds. And to the very congenial ladies I repeatedly encounter in The Waiting Room—my very stiff competition—see you soon.

Afterword

Bad Auditions

I met Julia Duffy in person a few years ago when she came in to audition for a play I was casting for The Alley Theater in Houston Texas. I was very familiar with her work in Film and Television. I was a huge fan of her brilliant comic portrayal of Stephanie Vanderkellen on *Newhart* and then as Allison Sugarbaker in *Designing Women*. I had not, however, had the opportunity to see her stage work, although I knew she had a respectable Theater resume. I have had many experiences with actors who are mostly known for their work in TV and Film. I must admit that I had a preconceived expectation based on my past experiences with LA actors. Honestly, I was expecting her to deliver a small cinematic read with lots of paraphrasing and not much preparation. I was not expecting the powerhouse of intelligence and connection to the role that she brought into the room that day. She was prepared, respectful of the text and clearly had done her homework. She was connected to the character, not only emotionally, but vocally and physically. She used the room to her advantage. She found humor where others did not, but most of all, there was a comfort and confidence that can only come from a love of auditioning and commitment to the craft.

I didn't get to cast her in that particular production, but the seed was planted. I made it my mission to cast her in something. Shortly thereafter, I did. It was a new play for The Huntington Theater in Boston. And not

111

long after that production, I cast her again in a play here at Playwrights Horizons in New York.

When Julia contacted me and asked me to contribute an Afterword to a book she was writing about the art of auditioning, it was in the middle of a snowstorm, and the office was closed due to the weather. This seemed like the perfect snow day read. I sat on my couch and dug in. In my career, I have read many books on navigating the audition process. Many are entertaining, but thin. Some are informative, but pretty dense.

This one is both entertaining and informative. Rarely are these books written by those making their living on the other side of the table from me. I imagined casting directors everywhere enthusiastically nodding their heads thinking here is a book that "gets it right." Julia's decades of experience are chronicled in a well-written series of anecdotes that are a gift to actors of any level. Her ponderings and conclusions result in expert storytelling filled with cautionary wisdom and advice.

"How could I have done it differently?" Julia questions her specific audition experiences over the years that didn't yield a desired result; from dealing with the purgatory of audition waiting rooms to the heaven of booking the job. These stories are frank and sharply funny. She confesses the "utter unfairness of it all," but makes suggestions on how to engage your auditioners and maintain your power and dignity.

Other chapters deal with difficult directors and the frustration of being pigeon-holed. How do you flip those preconceived judgments about you and use them to your advantage? There is advice on how to sharpen comic chops through improvisation classes and thereby spark your spontaneity. She even dives

BAD AUDITIONS

into the art of making an audition tape that pops and engages the viewer.

It is my desire that all who read this book will be inspired and empowered to love their calling and to never stop evolving as an artist. As Julia says, you must embrace the power of the word "yes," be courageous with your choices, and learn to love auditions. I always say, an audition is a chance to act. For 10 minutes you've got the part. The audition is not an opportunity to get a job. It is the job.

Alaine Alldaffer

Alaine Alldaffer is the Casting Director for Playwright's Horizons. Credits include Clybourne Park [PWH and Broadway], Grey Gardens, [Broadway and PWH], Circle Mirror Transformation [Artios Award], Present Laughter [Artios Award] with Victor Garber for The Huntington and Roundabout Theaters, and as of this writing the musical Far From Heaven, with Kelli O'Hara and Steven Pasquale. She also casts for regional theaters, including Berkeley Rep and ACT in San Francisco, Arena Stage in D.C., Boston's Huntington Theater, The Alley in Houston, and the Williamstown and Humana Theater Festivals, as well as the Women's Project Theater in NYC. TV credits include associate casting for *Monk* and *ED* and casting director for ABC's *Knights of Prosperity* aka *Let's Rob Mick Jagger.*

About The Author

Julia Duffy began her career in her hometown of Minneapolis, auditioning for—and sometimes getting roles in—summer stock and community theater. She graduated from the American Academy of Dramatic Arts in New York and began her professional career doing soap operas and theater. She appeared on Broadway in *Once in a Lifetime* at Circle-in-the-Square, and has worked in regional theater regularly—the Pasadena Playhouse, Laguna Playhouse, The Huntington in Boston, St. Louis Rep, and the Kennedy Center in Washington D.C. Theater credits include *The Little Foxes, The Heiress, Guess Who's Coming to Dinner, Curse of the Starving Class, Three Sisters, Richard III, Twelfth Night, The Merry Wives of Windsor,* and *Rancho Viejo* at Playwright's Horizons in New York. She is best known for playing Stephanie in *Newhart*, a role she played for 7 seasons, earning 7 Emmy Award nominations, plus Golden Globe and American Comedy Award nominations. She has been a regular on several other series and has many guest roles, mini-series and TV movie appearances to her credit. Most recently she has been seen in recurring roles on Showtime's *Shameless* and HBO's *Looking*, as well as roles on *Key and Peele, Drake and Josh,* the Coen brother's *Intolerable Cruelty* and *Scream Queens*. She currently resides, and auditions in, both New York and

Julia Duffy

Los Angeles with her husband actor/writer Jerry Lacy. They have two children, Kerry Lacy and Danny Lacy.